21st Century Junior Library

FARM ANIMALS
DUCKS

by Cecilia Minden

CHERRY LAKE PUBLISHING * ANN ARBOR, MICHIGAN

CHERRY
LAKE
Publishing

Published in the United States of America by Cherry Lake Publishing
Ann Arbor, Michigan
www.cherrylakepublishing.com

Content Adviser: Laurie Rincker, Assistant Professor of Agriculture, Eastern Kentucky University

Photo Credits: Page 4, ©Photowitch/Dreamstime.com; cover and page 6, ©iStockphoto.com/ ping69; cover and page 8, ©iStockphoto.com/jimkruger; cover and page 10, ©Dhoxax, used under license from Shutterstock, Inc.; page 12, ©iStockphoto.com/Devonyu; page 14, ©Shantell photographe, used under license from Shutterstock, Inc.; cover and page 16, ©iStockphoto.com/ RapidEye; page 18, ©Silvia Bogdanski, used under license from Shutterstock, Inc.; page 20, ©Flashon Studio, used under license from Shutterstock, Inc.

LIBRARY OF CONGRESS CATALOGING-IN-PUBLICATION DATA
Minden, Cecilia.
  Farm animals: Ducks / by Cecilia Minden.
    p. cm.—(21st century junior library)
  Includes bibliographical references and index.
  ISBN-13: 978-1-60279-546-4
  ISBN-10: 1-60279-546-0
  1. Ducks—Juvenile literature. I. Title. II. Title: Ducks. III. Series.
  SF505.3.M56 2009
  636.5'97—dc22   2009005033

Cherry Lake Publishing would like to acknowledge the work of
The Partnership for 21st Century Skills.
Please visit www.21stcenturyskills.org for more information.

CONTENTS

Ducks are often afraid of people, but some ducks get used to them.

Who Says Quack?

Is there a duck pond at your local park? Many people like to feed bread to ducks. The ducks seem to like it. But bread is bad for them. Do you know why? Let's find out as we learn more about ducks.

Male wood ducks have bright, eye-catching colors. Can you tell which duck is the drake?

Just Ducky

There are many kinds of ducks. They come in many different colors. **Drakes** are male ducks. Females are called **hens** or ducks. Drakes are usually more colorful than hens. Hens need to blend in with nature. This helps them hide from **predators**. Blending in also helps the hen protect her eggs.

Using feathers in the nest keeps the nest soft and warm.

A hen lays a **clutch** of eggs. There are between 6 and 12 eggs in most clutches. The hen sits on the eggs until they **hatch**.

Baby ducks are called **ducklings**. The hen leads the ducklings to water soon after birth. Many ducklings can swim within a day after being born.

Ducklings stay close to their mother. She protects them and teaches them how to find food.

The drake pays no attention to his ducklings. The hen watches over them. She teaches them to search for food. Ducks can fly when they are about 2 months old. Then they are on their own.

Think!

Ducks don't walk like people. They **waddle**. Ducks are very good swimmers. Can you figure out why they can swim so well? Hint: Think about a duck's feet. What do they look like? How are they different from other animals' feet?

This hungry mallard is dabbling.

If It Looks Like a Duck . . .

There are many kinds of ducks. Mallards are one kind of duck. Mallards are **dabblers**. They dip their heads into the water. Their tails point up into the air. This is how dabbling ducks reach for food. Other ducks find food in different ways. Some swim and dive under water for food.

People use down to make blankets or coats that are extra warm.

Ducks have a special **gland** near their tails. It produces oil. Ducks rub the oil on their feathers. This makes their feathers waterproof. Water rolls off feathers when they are oily. Ducks also have a layer of feathers called **down**. Down keeps ducks warm.

Look!

Look at pictures of different kinds of ducks. What colors are the ducks? How big are they? How are some ducks alike? In what ways are they different? Looking closely at animals helps us learn more about them.

Ducks should know how to find their own food.

No Bread for You!

Many people like to give bread to ducks. But bread does not give ducks the nutrition they need. It only makes them feel full. They stop looking for healthy food. Ducks can die from eating people food. They also learn to count on strangers to feed them. That is not a good thing.

Duck meat can be part of a healthy meal.

Do people raise ducks? Yes! Duck eggs may be kept at **hatcheries**. The ducks can be sent to special farms after they hatch. They receive healthy food. They can dig for worms and bugs. There are safe places to sleep. These farmers raise ducks to sell. Some people buy ducks as pets. Others like to eat duck eggs or duck meat.

You can find new and surprising facts about ducks at the library.

Now do you know why you shouldn't feed bread to ducks? Check out your local library. Find more books about these interesting birds. Look online, too. Ask an adult to help. There is still more to learn about ducks!

Make a Guess!

There are many kinds of ducks. They live in many places. Guess how many types of ducks live around the world. Where can you find the answer? The library is a good place to start. Was your guess correct?

GLOSSARY

clutch (KLUHCH) a group of eggs

dabblers (DAB-lurz) ducks that search for food by tipping their heads into the water and pointing their tails in the air

down (DOUN) soft fluffy feathers

drakes (DRAYKSS) male ducks

ducklings (DUHK-lings) baby ducks

gland (GLAND) an organ in the body that produces chemicals or liquids

hatch (HACH) to break out of an egg and be born

hatcheries (HACH-er-eez) places where eggs are hatched

hens (HENZ) female ducks

predators (PRED-uh-turz) animals that hunt other animals for food

waddle (WAHD-uhl) to walk using short steps while rocking from side to side

FIND OUT MORE

BOOKS

Endres, Hollie. *Ducks*. Minneapolis: Bellwether Media, 2008.

Royston, Angela. *Duck*. New York: DK Publishing, 2007.

WEB SITES

Animal Planet—Duck

animal.discovery.com/birds/duck/
For more information about ducks

Smithsonian National Zoological Park—Kids' Farm: Ducks

nationalzoo.si.edu/Animals/ KidsFarm/InTheBarn/Ducks/
Find fun facts and a link about caring for ducks

INDEX

ABOUT THE AUTHOR

Cecilia Minden, PhD, is a literacy consultant and author of many books for children. She lives with her family near Chapel Hill, North Carolina. Cecilia would like to thank Dara Cupp-Davulcu for her research help with this series. She promises not to give bread to ducks at the pond!